THE SHAPE OF THE WAVE

POEMS BY LEANNA GASKINS

AN OLD LEOPARD (2015)

TRAINS AND COTTONWOOD SEEDS (2018)

THE SHAPE OF THE WAVE (2022)

The Shape of the Wave

Poems by

Leanna Gaskins

Vinland Books

San Francisco ● *London*

International Standard Book Number: 979-8-9866346-0-9

Library of Congress Control Number: 2022943638

First published 2022 by
Vinland Books
2443 Fillmore Street
San Francisco, CA 94115

Vinland Books
27, Old Gloucester Street
London WC1N 3XX

www.vinlandbooks.com

1 3 5 7 9 10 8 6 4 2

In memory of

Bob and Anna Gaskins

who sailed many seas together

CONTENTS

THE SHAPE OF THE WAVE

I

The shape of the wave
Is the shape of the ocean.
The shape and curve,
The lilt and turn,
Where the wave arches over,
Is the shape of ocean itself,
In white caps
And endless turning.
As the thunder of surf
Shouts power and grace,
The tall waves dance
Across miles of water,
With a shout of exultation.
As the subtle colors
Of blue and gray and green
Shade the waves along the shore,
So also out in the deep,
The blue, the green
Color the vast expanse.
Writ small, writ large,
Alike the form and substance,
The wonder of great waters.

SEASONS

.

II

Clouds lined westward across the sky
Echo the lines of furrows in the fields.
And watercolor edges of the clouds
Are likewise mirrored in plant-softened edges
Of straight and narrow furrows below.
The sky is sullen, and the wind's sharp edges
Show a harsher side of this October scene.
Winter may not wait until December.
Perhaps the fringe of its shawl
Sweeps over us today,
Flung over a shoulder
And sliding away.
Take warning, the barrier of summer
Is breached, and all the lines
Slant westward.

III

Now the sky lowers,
And the old peach trees
Bow beneath the snow,
Their branches gnarled and dark
Beneath the whiteness.
It is the quiet end
Of the season of growing.
Now by the side
Of the cold river,
They wait and rest.
The dark, still sky
Abides with them
In winter's habitation.

IV

August,
And looking across the fields,
We wish it were still April.
The crops are meager,
And we wish we could
Start over.
But the year slides by,
And mornings grow darker.
The crops that we see,
We must accept and harvest,
And so make do
With August and September,
And what we can glean
From the harvest of the year.

V

Tumbleweeds pile up against the fence,
And winter's coming.
Have to pull them down and burn them,
Before the snow falls.
Drifting in among their interlaced branches,
It would overwhelm and topple that fence.
So we walk the fences.
And the countryside is dotted
With bonfires consuming
Those incursive nomads,
Pitching their tents along the borders
Of our fields.

VI

There is no warmth now.
I came too late for that.
Dawdling in the gallery,
Among the white columns
Of the aspens,
To admire one more
Painted sunset,
And listen to one more
River symphony.
Until the lights were dimmed,
And the doors closed,
Closed on sun and warmth.
Now here I am,
Where warmth is shut out,
And only winter's cold awaits.

VII

ANNALS OF COLD

Night in the old farmhouse,
Out on the prairie,
Relic from earlier times.
It had no central heat,
Only the coal stove in the parlor.
Sleeping upstairs, not used to the cold,
We huddled together,
Right up against the chimney.
In the morning, we squealed
At the shock of cold,
And ran downstairs
To the warmth of the kitchen stove.

Night in the mountain cabin,
Curled in the blankets,
Hanging over the side of the bed,
To catch what warmth
Filtered up from the old steam heater.
In the morning, shivering in the cold,
And opening the door to find
The porch all barred with icicles.

Christmas Eve in the old church,
Cold despite a big congregation,
We shiver and envy

The priest's warm vestments.
When the service ends, we walk home,
Beneath an icy moon
And shivering stars.
Hearing the refrain, "Gaudete, Gaudete!"
But eager for the warmth of home.

VIII

Summer sits there,
At the edge of the meadow,
With somnolent sun
Casting long shadows
Over the fading grasses.
Summer waits while
The last abundance
Of blossom and fruit
Passes by and is blessed,
And recedes into shadow.
Summer sits there,
And fall is gathering
The last grapes.
Leaves are already
Golden and drifting
Along the meadow.
And fall flings the acorns
Across the meadow grass
To lie at summer's feet.

IX

Sing me a song of the river,
Of bright days and cool nights,
And the water always flowing,
Past the changes and the sorrows,
Flowing on.
Sing me a song of springtime,
Aspens in leaf and small birds
Winging along the cliffs.
Last of the ice dislodged,
Floating on.
Sing me a song of summer,
Lazy sunshine and buzzing voices
Of bees and all little peoples
That summer brings to the river,
Dancing on.
Sing me a song of autumn,
Golden leaves and golden days,
The last of the summer songs ending.
Songs of winter beginning,
With the mists among the cliff tops,
Flowing on.

TIME AND TIMES

X

Today the sky is heavy and dark,
Filled with ash,
Like acrid snowflakes,
Falling across our homes and streets.
And every flake is a sob.
For each one is the last remnant
Of someone's total loss.
Over there on the other side of the hills,
Fires eliminate lives and dreams.
And here they descend in ashes,
Silvery flakes falling around us,
Each one forged in anguish.

XI

They call it ordinary time.
And the casual speech of the years
Has sometimes made it "ornery."
So, ornery folk, ornery time.
And indeed time is both,
Ordinary, undistinguished,
And ornery, troublesome.
And we are all ordinary,
Creatures like time itself.
Bit by bit, layer by layer,
We are formed like a cliff.
An ordinary time sort of structure,
Ornery too, and stubborn it is,
Taking eons of ordinary time
To become its ornery self.

XII

GOLD SPIKE DAY

On this day,
One hundred and fifty years ago,
They finished the transcontinental,
The railroad of dream,
Uniter of states,
Mother of the West.
And there they rejoiced,
And telegraphed "Done".
They drank champagne,
And some probably danced
In the Utah sun.
As they set aside the thought
That tomorrow
They must run the trains.

XIII

4:14, and the last train
Whistles off and departs
Into the darkness,
Carrying the last weary riders
Through the transition
Of night sliding into day.
The starlight is fading into
The first intimation of dawn.
5:26, and the first train
Stands waiting while
Four or five riders
Climb sleepily into the cars.
Dawn climbs the east,
And the train climbs to meet it,
Beginning another day's runs.
Around the cycle
Of inward and outward,
Of end and beginning,
A new day emerges perpetually
From the shell of the old.

XIV

SEIS DE MAYO

Wake up, it's morning!
Time to go to work.
No holiday today.
Some people drank too much
Yesterday, and today there's
Just the hangover.
Some people listened too long
Yesterday to speeches,
Standing in the sun,
Letting the lies beguile them.
And today, there's
Just the hangover.
Drinkers and listeners,
With befuddled heads,
Today there's no clear vision,
Just the hangover.

XV

Watching that scene in the morning,
The young mother taking the hand
Of her child going off to school
For the first time.
And then you look back,
From more than forty years
Of wilderness wandering,
And wish you could remember
How that felt,
When your mother
Put you on the school bus
For the first time.
How you wish you had looked back
To see the tears in her eyes,
And the love in her smile.

XVI

You see, that's Mountain Time.
Past the limits of prairie,
Into the upslope,
That's Mountain Time.
That's the high, clear tone of song
In the morning sunrise,
And the softly shimmering light
Of the moon on the cliffside.
That's evening song falling
With falling leaves in the twilight.
A time to wait in the silence
For moonrise above the cliff.
Time to sleep in soft darkness
Where time stops for a bit
And waits without impatience
For the morning that comes
In Mountain Time.

XVII

Shakespeare is hiding behind his mask,
And all the prophets turn away.
They refuse to speak.
So the year ends without an oracle.
We wined and dined
In the halls of deception.
No writing on the wall to warn us,
But the light drained away.
The music of feasting
Turned to alarm bells shrieking.
And somewhere, potent in the darkness,
Samson already brings down the walls.

XVIII

This is a slow dance.
Frenetic twists and turns forgotten,
We sway silently,
And pace solemnly,
Not cheek to cheek,
Nor even palm to palm.
Learning the steps to this
Slow dancing too,
Strange and confusing though they are.
Yet we keep the memory,
Heart and muscle retaining
All those lighter steps we learned.
So when this dance is over,
When this dark music is stilled,
We can dance again in joy.

IMAGES

XIX

My old copper bracelet,
A link to long ago,
Worn again tonight,
Brings back the memories
Of those days of work and longing.
And that store where they hid
Naughty magazines under the counter.
But that bracelet was visible,
Bright and beautiful in the case.
And so, one day,
Gathering my courage,
And the whole week's earnings,
Paid cash hard-earned,
And walked away with it.
Now, when it rests on my wrist,
Now, when it's easy to buy
Most anything that's wanted,
It's that day I remember.
And all the years between
Melt into the shape
Of my old copper bracelet.

XX

They took the old house away,
That sturdy old farmhouse,
Where we lived and played as children.
And we sorrow to see the blankness
Where that solid old place stood.
We wonder what happens,
What becomes of an old house,
Torn from its long mooring
And sent somewhere,
Carrying its memories to someplace,
Some unknown place.
Will its memories fit and take root,
Or will it all just wither and die?
Torn from its garden,
Where it prospered so long,
And fostered its families,
What will become of it now,
Stripped of all that it was,
Of all that it meant?

XXI

The work of their hands endures.
It looks so fragile,
The crochet open and delicate,
The embroidery perfect,
With stitches so small and smooth.
How could it survive all the years,
All the careless treatment?
And yet, behind the fragile beauty
Is strength and the power
Of thread and thought interwoven.
We cannot now match it.
Looking at their work,
We just sigh and wish
We could have learned.

XXII

Way out west.
So the photo is labeled.
And there we stand,
By the roadside,
Gazing across the vastness,
So western a landscape
That one would not wonder
To see war-painted Indians
Riding over the hill.
Out here, where cities seem
Not just far away,
But almost far-fetched.
Standing there, says the label,
Waiting for a train.
There beneath so western a sky,
Inhabiting so western a dream,
Between sky and endless plains,
Looking for the link.
Way out west,
Waiting for a train.

XXIII

Happiness hung out in Grandma's kitchen,
Nestled between the tulip patterned curtains
And the battered old table
That had held so many feasts,
So many family gatherings.
Happiness was centered
In Grandma's loving presence,
Her gentle, knowing hands
That always tended us,
Body and soul.
Always we were drawn there,
To the warmth of true home.
Coming back from all directions
To that center,
Where happiness taught us
The world held no more beautiful place
Than Grandma's kitchen.

XXIV

The glow of the kerosene lamp
In Grandfather's house
Lit our evenings and mornings.
No electric bulbs lighted our way,
So the old lamps steadily
Kept darkness at bay.
There by the lamp's light,
We ate our meals and sat to read,
And went to bed cheered
By the softness of the flame.
The old house is gone,
And the lamps with it.
But the calm glow of their light
Still shines in our memory.
Across the years and miles,
It keeps the darkness at bay
In our city life.

XXV

That was a brick road indeed,
There where I lived,
There where I did quite a bit of what
They call growing up.
It was neither yellow,
Nor magical at all.
Just a city street,
Sometimes full of snow,
Sometimes running with rain water,
People coming and going.
And our house sat there,
The driveway connected us,
And our coming and going,
With that brick road.
Neither yellow nor magical,
But it took us where
We needed to go.

XXVI

They said there was a shop,
Somewhere on the other side of town,
Where they served leopards
With food and drink appropriate,
And cozy places to lie and sleep.
They said it was a place where
Leopards could at last be accepted,
Maybe even loved.
It must have been well hidden though,
For I never found it.
But those captivating images
Are vivid even now.

XXVII

The sun slants in from the west.
Its light blesses everything with gold.
All the surfaces and all the faces
Are enriched with the glory of light.
No one notices.
The child at the table across the way
Looks into the light without flinching,
Engrossed in the game she is playing.
And all through the room, the faces
Are closed to the splendor of sunlight,
As over the vastness to westward,
Without regard to who sees or ignores,
It floods the whole prairie and city,
Extravagant gift of an extravagant God.

THE UNFINISHED

XXVIII

Thinking about all the unfinished places,
Where we went and did not clearly
Understand what they were.
Those places we chose with limited vision,
And went there before we could see
What they were.
And so the unfinished vision
Traveled back with us,
And stays with us,
Lodged deep in memory.
We wish we could go back
And finish the places
Whose truth we did not know.

XXIX

A frosty morning at the dawn of time.
And there we were,
The high school drill team,
Practicing the steps and turns
For our performance.
The sky above was blue and clear,
But we were all bound
To the effort to step just so.
There in the cold morning sun,
We all learned something.
And after all these years,
It still is not clear
Just what we learned.

XXX

Sitting in my friend's kitchen,
With a slice of her mother's apple pie,
Long ago when we listened
To voices on the radio.
Coming home from school
To sit with my friend and listen
To the saga of the Lone Ranger,
And there in the kitchen,
Hearing a tale unfinished,
With drama unsettled,
And danger left unresolved.
The day faded and sent me home,
And nothing ever again brought back
A chance to hear the answer,
To know the outcome.
All the long years have left
That saga yet unfinished.

XXXI

The old restaurant was there for years.
It wasn't much,
Just a diner sort of place.
But always there were people inside,
And cars in the little parking lot.
Then the paint shop next door
Went out of business,
And a Trader Joe's moved in.
Right away there was a stream of traffic,
But none of it stopped
There at the restaurant.
Thus time passed,
And they were passed by.
So the old place was closed,
Sold for a high price,
To be replaced by a high rise.
Now it's empty and forlorn,
With peeling paint and boarded windows.
No building to replace its emptiness,
For the high rise is on hold.
And the poor old restaurant
Has also lost its hold.

XXXII

Coming through the air,
From all that strange distance,
Through sky and downward slant,
Into a place never seen before.
Riding the currents
Of air and time and circumstance,
And finding oneself among
Unfamiliar, unexpected images.
Walking about there,
And trying to fathom
The currents of air and time
That brought one there,
And then, turning away
Into the air and silence,
Without answer or connection.

XXXIII

The end of the page
Is torn off,
And the rest of the story
Is lost.
What it might have been,
We shall never know.
Now the page turns,
And a new story emerges.
We may well wish
We might have kept
The older story.
But the page is torn off,
And it is gone.

VISIONS AND VERITIES

XXXIV

He looked like an old friend,
The man who sat down
At the table next to ours –
With his long, grizzled beard,
And a tie-dyed scarf around his neck.
And we who came of age
Among those symbols,
Smile gently and remember
All the long roads we've all walked.
Looking at him, we may wonder
Whether he teaches
At the nearby college.
He seemed an academic somehow.
But whatever his work and life,
He looked like an old friend
From long ago.

XXXV

Ursula K. LeGuin

The great teller of stories
Is now herself a story.
Remembered, memorialized,
By many who knew her,
But mostly,
Her tale is stored up,
Along with those wonderful
Tales year by year she told,
By the fireside of our imagination.
In us, her story lives,
We who sat with her
And savored again and again
The magical images
That she, like the Lady of Shalott,
Wove from mirrored vision.

XXXVI

The store was gone long ago,
But the sign is still there.
Mysterious and alluring,
It reads Red Lantern Antiques.
How can empty windows and dusty shelves
Conjure visions of hidden treasure?
Yet the slant of the street light
Raises ghosts of beauty long gone.
And always, passing by there,
You wonder what it was.
What did they sell?
Such an intriguing name –
And nothing left to give a clue.
The store has been empty
As long as we remember.
What did it once contain?
And did it ever
Live up to its beautiful,
Mysterious name.

XXXVII

The Psalm says,
"Your clothes are scented
With aloes and cloves."
Mine are scented rather
With snow and rocks,
And sometimes maybe,
With creosote and smoke,
All the harsher scents
Of railroad and canyon.
They are the scents
Of life as we live it here.
No languid evenings
Draped in clove scented robes.
The road and the rocks,
And the moonrise over the mesa,
These are the scents,
Red rock and snowfall,
Which cling to my clothes.

XXXVIII

In rust-colored shadows,
The old factories and houses
Fade into the dark.
Stately old brick buildings,
Streaked with rust,
Like the tracks of tears.
Their windows, boarded up,
Mourn the emptiness within.
Memories breed only melancholy,
Without substance to build again.
Somewhere across the fields,
A train whistle sounds warning
At a seldom used crossing.
The railroad still runs through,
But the trains no longer stop here.
The old depot sees only
A flock of mourning doves,
Their sorrowing cry following the trains.
They soon rise and fly away,
Like trains and people,
Without a backward glance.

XXXIX

KERRY

Folded in there among the memories
Are all the bright mornings,
The quiet conversations.
All the sweetness of laughter
And family tales
Folded like yeast in the batter.
The sunniness of talk and smiles,
The sharing of times and travels –
All the things we knew
And gave each other,
Completed in knowing
Each other's experience.
All are folded together
Into the perfect image
Of our times together.

XL

From down here beside the river,
Those old dwellings,
Empty these long years,
Glow in the sunrise.
Like some fabled city of palaces,
Nearly unreachable now,
They awake the imagination,
Seeming to shimmer in the glow.
It becomes easy to wonder
What our cities would look like
If perched beneath immense arches
Of glowing red stone,
Approachable only through
The bright shimmer of air.

XLI

MY MOTHER'S BIRTHDAY

She would be 103 today.
Thinking about that,
The numbers seem too small,
Too puny to hold
The full scope of what
That concept contains.
Born on the raw edge
Of the twentieth century,
On the unhemmed fabric
Of a frontier just coalescing
Into a sober, settled thing.
That place and time
Are now so remote as to seem
Like some sort of myth.
She was there, growing up
In ways none of us, coming after,
Could ever know.
And all through her life,
She carried that ever expanding scope.

XLII

A good night to be home.
And don't you know
It's a more loved comfort,
These quiet rooms, calm and still,
When the cold swirls by outside,
And all the town shivers.
So good to leave the windy darkness,
Sit by the fire and sip from old stories,
And rejoice in the uncountable
Wealth of quiet and warmth.
A good night to be home.

XLIII

The elegant beauty
Of the dishes on the table,
The perfect curve
Of one into the next,
The clever, or perhaps
Spontaneous reflection
Of the shape of
Flowers in the vase.
Yes, and the mountain,
Perfect slope beyond the window.
Calm and reflective,
The shapes and the colors,
And thus so perfect
That one does not at once
Recognize the art
That has so carefully
Produced them.

XLIV

They say she used to sing there,
In the bar called Metropolitan Collective,
A place no longer to be found
In any city where
Internet search can go.
She used to be the luminous
Star of that place,
More metropolitan than any one
Of the hipsters who came
From all around to hear her sing.
And she is gone,
Her voice is lost,
Somewhere among the streets and alleys,
The metropolitan abyss,
A collective of silences.
But once, long ago, they say,
She used to sing there.

PRAYER AND PRAISE

XLV

Oh, to stand with Elijah
On the mountainside,
And hear that sound
Of infinite silence.
Beyond all our imagining,
The silent voice of the One Speaker.
All through life, we must listen,
Hoping there might be
The faintest whisper,
And we, attuned to silence,
Might catch, just for a moment,
That perfect sound,
Beyond which, perhaps,
No ear can hear again,
No voice can dare to speak.

XLVI

The ones who were rejected
And left outside,
Wondering what they did wrong,
Looking with longing at the chosen ones,
And gazing at themselves in sorrow,
Wondering how they fell short –
Those ones whose struggle
Never seemed enough,
Whose merit always
Slipped below notice,
And their careful endeavor
Was always lost in the shuffle.
The ones who stood and waited,
And never made it to the head of the line,
These whose sad endurance
Went unnoticed until now,
The Shepherd of Souls calls forward.
He gives them the smile they never saw,
The pat on the back,
And the crown of victory.
And he says to them,
For all the universe to hear,
"Well done, good and faithful servants."

XLVII

They grow wild in the fields, she said.
We just gather them there.
The beautiful blossoms,
Delicate pinks and blues,
Shades of lavender among them,
Growing wild in the fields.
Their bounty of beauty
Is given without limit
To the hands of all
Who can see and know,
And come to gather the gift.
Like the bounty of the Father's love,
Growing wild in the universe.
There for whoever can see
And hear the Spirit
Saying, "Come."

XLVIII

Behold the infinite grace of God.
In the midst of His great work of salvation,
The work ordained
From before all creation,
Right there, He saw the details,
He recognized great need,
And He gave Elizabeth a child.
In the midst of the highest,
The holiest endeavor,
He saw her desolation,
And gave her a child.
All the high and mysterious work
Of incarnation and redemption
Is prefigured in this.
John the Baptist could have been born anywhere,
But the Lord God looked on barren Elizabeth,
And to her He gave that child.

XLIX

There is no room in there,
They said.
But we looked
And saw that the corners
Were unoccupied.
So we sent the seekers
To fill up the corners
And fill up the air
With prayer and praise.
And then they said,
There is no room at all.
And we looked again
And saw that the corridors
Were full of empty spaces.
The seekers came and filled them.
And now all the rooms
And corridors were filled
With songs of praise
And prayers for grace.
And don't you know
How glad we were
To fill those empty spaces.

L

She knew.
She was His mother.
And mothers always see more.
The stories hint of things
She must have seen.
And she always remembered
And pondered
Those things like the angel
Who said her child was from God.
And the shepherds who said the same.
So of course she knew.
And when at Cana
They ran out of wine,
Knowing He was there,
On the cusp of His revealing,
She said to the servants,
"Do whatever He says."
Because she knew.

LI

Sometimes what we hear
Is the music,
And we cannot write that.
So we just listen,
And rejoice in knowing
This is the voice,
Spoken as song,
That we always wait to hear.
Sometimes what we see
Is the sunlight,
And we cannot write that.
And so we stand,
Waiting in silence,
Hoping that in golden light
That voice will speak
Some words we can write.

LII

It is said
That there is a song
In the voids, the open spaces.
It is said
That if you listen,
You can hear the music,
That infinite harmony,
Created when the All Lord
Spoke the word of beginning,
And all the heavenly beings
Shouted and sang with joy.
And somehow that song,
Preserved in the fabric of creation,
Resides there, hidden
In secret voids of cave and vessel,
Until a receptive ear,
Seeking and listening,
Shall find, shall hear
The perfect melody
They sang on that day,
The beginning of creation.

CONNECTIONS

LIII

It's still stuck there,
A bit of residue left from cooking,
So long ago that the pots,
Hidden in sand and silt,
Have been lost for centuries.
But still it's stuck there,
In the corners at the bottom,
The last of what it was
They cooked and ate,
There beside the Nile,
Such a long time ago.
Long ages before anyone knew
How to make a thing like
A non-stick cooking pot.

LIV

Where are they going,
Walking on down past us?
That way is the desert.
No refuge there.
Here we sit in the oasis,
Calm and quiet,
With a table before us,
Holding wine and water,
Sheltered and serene.
Over there is just heat and dust,
And dark habitations.
Why don't they stay?
Where do they think they're going?
What makes that journey
Worth enduring?

LV

All the tales of lost mines,
The hidden, infinite variety
Of shining products
From the under earth,
Scattered everywhere,
And found by chance,
Then lost again.
Some remain lost
And form the vaporous legends
Of hidden desert treasure,
Like the sea dwelling sirens,
Drawing men to distraction and death.
Perhaps they are guarded by spirits
Of an inimical sort,
Whose cold night cry
Causes even the coyotes
To shudder and flee.

LVI

The rocket has completed its mission,
And now its impervious skin
Is reborn as cooking pans.
Their vitreous surfaces
Will face only the mild flames
Of cookstoves and grills.
No more the raucous scream of liftoff.
But yet,
Those mundane pans still carry
Something of the fiery ascents,
Some touch of blackness and stars,
Which maybe sometimes
We can taste.

LVII

Treat them gently, for they are
The last of those old artifacts,
The last remainder of the years
We lived in joy despite the lacks.
How fragile are the memories.
How easily the past is lost.
Treat gently those last curios
That tie us to the fading past.
How easy to let go, forget,
The years of learning and of growth.
Ask ourselves if we have yet
Arrived at something like the truth.
If we are honest, we shall see
We need the help of years and days.
So treat them gently, so that they
May stay with us,
Remind us thus,
We're learning still to find our ways.

LVIII

What does it mean,
The Forty Mile Desert?
Now, forty miles is nothing to cross,
Something we do every day without thinking.
But consider back then,
What a distance it was.
At the pace of the oxen,
The crossing was days long,
And water was nowhere
To be found on the way.
So think of the peril.
And think of the courage it took
To set out, knowing
What stood between
You and your goal,
Between you and survival.
Forty Mile Desert,
Like the way to the moon.

LIX

A wheel turned somewhere,
Silent revolution.
Maybe it was a spinning wheel,
Turning wool into thread,
Or flax into gold.
Maybe it was a great steel wheel,
Starting an engine,
And turning coal into flame
And water into steam.
Or maybe it was a tiny cog
In the clock,
Turning unnoticed seconds
Into measured hours and days.
Or maybe it was digital,
That hidden counting wheel
That changes April to May,
And this year to the next.
Somewhere, it turned,
And is turning again.

LX

Talatat, they call them.
The very word contains
The staccato sound
Of hammers on stone.
Talatat, the broken pieces
Of some king's ancient monument,
Rescued from where, heedless,
They were re-used, and now
Lined in rows and studied.
Now scholars devote their work
To reunite the broken legend,
To undo the hammer blows
That made them into talatat.

LXI

Ragged little lumps of clay,
Lying in the archeologist's hand,
Broken clay sealings
That bespeak a vast and thriving
Bureaucratic culture
All those ages ago.
Those official sealings from some --
Perhaps classified – document,
To read which,
The seal must be broken,
The code untangled,
Now lie in the sun.
After long sleep in darkness,
Long preserved by sand and dryness,
There they tell us again,
There is nothing much new
Under the sun.

LXII

Those red clay pots
Are everywhere to be found.
Going back to the dawn of history,
Or even pre-history.
Shaped to hold everyday needs,
No glamorous stone bowl,
Or golden goblet,
Just those ubiquitous
Red clay pots everywhere.
And you wonder whether,
If Leakey had dug a little deeper,
He might have found the remnants
Of Lucy's red clay pots.

WIND AND STORM

LXIII

Wind should be cool,
But this wind is hot.
No respite from this
Fierce pursuit.
The rustle of leaf and grass
Has the sound of
Crackling flame.
What should be comfort
Is branding torture.
Dust moves in it too,
Like ashes of a volcano.
Facing this wind,
You wouldn't blame Esau
If he sold his birthright
For a parcel of ice.

LXIV

Storm, are you coming?
They said you were,
And I've waited.
But the sky is placid blue.
Where are you lurking?
Are you like a leopard
Hiding up there
In the branches of the sky,
Waiting for me, unwary,
To step out and under your claws?
Or can it be that you
Chose instead to curl up,
Wrapped in warmth and dozing?
Until next time.

LXV

The light looked scorched
That day the fires began.
And seeing the color in the sky,
We knew with dread,
Disaster was coming.
Like steam from a volcano,
It colored the sunlight
And shook our assurance,
Like the faint tremor
That begins an earthquake.
Ominous foretaste
Of smoke and ruin to come.

LXVI

It converges on that vision.
The night in the storm,
Running for shelter,
With the road swept in water and wind.
The skies full of lightning,
And hail on all sides,
We ran hard to get through.
And the terror of storm remained,
Even in the refuge,
The hail tearing at the roof,
And cries of fear on every side.
It converges here now,
In the storm's fearsome darkness,
As in dark dread we wait and hope
This storm too may pass,
And leave us unharmed.

LXVII

I had to wash the wind off my hands,
And the water came away
Clear as crystal,
Yet full of the wild wind,
Somehow lodged there.
But the wind's reality
Remained behind.
It strayed into mind and heart,
Blowing ever stronger
Among the pillars and arches,
The inner structures
That house our being.
Oh wind, mysterious beauty,
Come back again into my hands.

LXVIII

STORM TRACK

All the sidings were plugged,
So they sent the first storm
On another route.
And then the yard was congested,
So the next one was held out
For quite a while.
And then, somewhere
There was a derailment,
And so the next incoming one
Had to go over Donner.
Now they say the sidings
Are plugged from here to the border.
Guess they'll all be funneled
Into Oregon.

LXIX

The songs of water and wind
Take the place of human voices,
When we for grief
Have not voice nor leave to sing,
And when we for joy
Have not depth or strength.
The songs of water and wind
Carry for us the longing.
Their deep and thrilling voices
Fill up the choir where we cannot stand.
The songs of flower and leaf
Join with those mighty voices,
And sing the softer and sweeter
Parts of the song,
Threading among the vast caroling
Of wave and wind and rain.

REFLECTIONS

LXX

I paid the price for that,
And if you want it,
You'll have to also
Pay the price.
I won't cling to that,
But if you want it,
You'll have to cling to that,
And pay the price.
It isn't anything
That couldn't always
Be bought and sold,
Wherever things are bought and sold.
I bought it once, but now
It isn't anything
That I would cling to.
So you can have it,
If you are foolish enough
To pay the price.

LXXI

Sitting there and listening
To the young doctor,
You know he has no idea
How far you came to see him.
Across the ice and tundra,
To sit here and wonder
Whether he can even see
The scars of walrus teeth
And years of trudging
Through ice canyons and endless cold.
Looking at his face, you know
He cannot see you.

LXXII

Here in the perspective of years,
I wonder what they
Must have said to each other,
At night when they talked about
What their daughter,
The one they'd lived with all the years,
Suddenly said she needed.
What did they see?
How did they understand
And come to terms with
This daughter of theirs,
Whose difference confronted them?
And I who was that daughter,
Only in this perspective of years
Am able to see enough
To wonder how they came to accept.
And how, past all the differences,
They always knew
How to give the love that ever,
Past all the changes,
Kept us whole.

LXXIII

AREA CODES

Those numbers written everywhere
Map the borders of state and country.
If you know the pattern,
You can read the motion,
The voices carried from there to here,
Residing in those quaint threesomes,
That chain distances to voice.
Old technology, living on,
From dial to button to screen,
Ubiquitous tie to origins
Of place and time.

LXXIV

The silence waited,
More patient than I.
And when I came finally,
Worn with the clamor,
It folded me kindly
Into its chamber,
Where even impatience
Is welcomed to home.

LXXV

We had a perfect summer that year.
With the family all together,
We roamed the high roads of Colorado.
There, we reacquainted ourselves
With sunlit peaks and wide vistas,
And we sang the songs of summer
In canyon and mountain meadow.
The clouds were always just passing,
And we gathered memories,
Along with river rocks and tokens.
Evening in the shadow of the cliffs
Became morning in blazing sunrises,
And the peace of mountain time
Was always with us.
Ah yes, it was a perfect summer.
And fortunately, we did not know
It was the last.

LXXVI

Shall I wait?
The leopard said to the mountain,
As morning was coming
High on the peak.
Yes, time will pass,
Said the mountain.
And the leopard sat to wait.
Shall I wait?
The leopard said to the river,
As the ice was slowly melting,
And the water began to flow.
Yes, we are moving,
Said the river.
So the leopard sat,
Quiet in the sun.
Shall I wait?
The leopard asked the starlight,
As the curve of the sky
Turned westward.
Yes, wait, said the stars.
Tomorrow will soon be here.

LXXVII

Balanced on the rim of the crater,
The crow and I,
And a rock between us.
In silence we wait.
I for the sunrise.
The crow for who knows what.
And the rock as they always do.
The mountain is still.
Perhaps it waits too,
With its precipitous crater
Somnolent in the dimness
Of early morning light and shadow.
And now the sun
Leaps over the far peaks,
Flames across the crater rim
Like fresh magma.
And the crow, just as sudden,
Flares into the air.
His wing flap disturbs
The rock's balance,
And over the side it tumbles,
Soon lost among the army of stones
Gathered below there.
Now there is only me,
Shading eyes from sun glare,
Balanced alone on the rim.

LANGUAGE

LXXVIII

Snippets of language
From various places,
Learned and carried,
But never really absorbed,
Drifting with us through the years
And the changes,
Never abandoned,
But never renewed.
What did they mean
When they took root inside us?
What did they try to give or create?
It was just time and the chance
Where they found us.
Now what of all they gave us remains?
Snippets of language
That should have blossomed,
A few random words,
A phrase here and there –
Trimmings and tailings
From the mine.

LXXIX

She loved what she taught,
And she struggled to teach us.
Day after day, in the limits she found,
Working to give us the knowledge
And share her love of that knowledge.
Even though we were too foolish to know –
Too foolish and eager to be on our way.
And so we missed that great chance,
All she had to give.
Yet she never faltered,
And always believed
That somehow the old language,
The Latin she loved, would live.
Looking back on those days of grace,
When learning was possible even for us,
Who never perceived the gift we were offered,
How precious even now,
The bits and pieces we did keep.

LXXX

Sometimes we write blindly,
By feel in the darkness,
Not even sure how much
Will be readable.
The words cry so within
That we can have no rest
Until we assuage their voices.
Then when we return to read
In the daylight,
Sometimes we find,
With relief and wonder,
That those urgent words
Came forth somehow
In lucid calm.

LXXXI

The fold is familiar.
That's where they always
Folded the pages
And bound the old codex.
And because we know
That familiar fold,
We can seek and find there
The occasional hidden word,
Nearly lost in the stitches.
Likewise, there in the fold
And the stitches
That hold the universe
Bound into a readable codex,
Sometimes right there
We can find a hidden word.

LXXXII

Gather the words, new and old.
Seed the cloud with them.
And hope falling rain of syllables
Will renew the fields of language.
Translate nothing.
Let the words reside there in ether
As uttered.
That, hearing the cadence,
Ear and brain may image,
And so receive each meaning,
Like raindrops descending.

LXXXIII

Three rocks lying on the stair,
Evenly spaced, but different
In size and color and form.
What do you suppose
They might signify?
There they lie on a city street,
Along a row of houses.
Did somebody place them
To leave a message
Of some sort?
Or was it just a whim
Of someone who picked them up
Along the way?
Were they meant as a gift
For someone who lives there?
Who knows what coded message
They might carry, if only
One could read
The language of rocks.

LXXXIV

The sun has written
In dots and dashes
On the window shade.
Those fiery lines of telegraph code
Surely must mean something.
But the language
Is not one we know.
Sun, what did you write there?
Is there a translation
For those enigmatic
Dots and dashes?

OKEANOS

LXXXV

Beautiful cold water,
Flowing dark and deep
Beneath the bridge.
Mysterious, changing blue,
And waves tipped with moonlight.
Old dark sea,
Who can comprehend
The years gathered there,
Flowing onward?
We cross above on frail constructs,
And mostly never think
What power rolls beneath,
There where the bridge strides.
But the cold, beautiful sea
Flows under and out,
Carrying all the years with it
Into the unfathomable deep.

LXXXVI

There they stand,
The myriads of stars arrayed
Across the little bit of sky,
The strip we can see.
There they witness,
Night and day,
Seen and unseen,
That He who made our seas and shores
Also made these seas,
Deep beyond our measuring,
With waves breaking
On shores we cannot know.

LXXXVII

That's an infinity pool,
For real,
There where the sea slides off
Into the blue of sky,
Flowing among the stars,
Without border or limit.
That's an infinity pool,
Full of mystery and glamor
And the fitful gleam
Of starlight and moonlight.
Infinite reaches
Beyond all imagining,
That's an infinity pool.

LXXXVIII

Deep blue.
The sky darkens past sunset,
With the kind of blue
That only comes at twilight.
Calm and still,
The sky collects itself,
And draws the last little clouds
Across the horizon.
Soon the stars and the moon
Will populate that sky.
Now it is just the serene
Deep blue.
And the ocean too,
Deep blue.
Cold waters sweeping
Out past the horizon.
Full of power and mystery,
Surging past the shore
And on out to where
The eye cannot follow.
Deep blue
Of sonorous waves
And quiet sky.

LXXXIX

The sea is always there,
The Okeanos, the great depth,
The encircler.
Surging, singing,
Always in our awareness,
Part of our very bodies
And part of all our days.
Seaward, songward,
So we pass our days,
Headed always to the shore,
Always to the great deep,
The waves breaking endless,
And the vast form of the water,
Shining out to the sky.

INDEX OF TITLES AND FIRST LINES

About the Author

LEANNA GASKINS spent her early years on a Kansas wheat farm without electricity, gas, or inside plumbing. She went to school in Dodge City and then to the University of Kansas, transferring when invited to a program in economics at Rampart College, in the mountains of Colorado.

She moved to Los Angeles where she spent several years and married. She graduated as a Regents Scholar from the University of California, Berkeley, and earned a Ph.D. in Linguistics there, applying modern formal linguistic theory to the ancient Egyptian language written in hieroglyphic, which she also taught to a generation of UC Berkeley Egyptology students.

Anticipating the coming importance of personal computers, she moved to Silicon Valley to join very early startup software companies as a teacher, writer, and manager of writing groups. During this same period she researched railroad history in travels over all the western states, and was one of a small team who rebuilt and restored the long-dormant Southern Pacific 2472 steam locomotive.

She retired very early and moved with her husband to central London where they lived and studied for ten years, after which they returned to live in San Francisco. She has written poetry since her early college years.

www.ingramcontent.com/pod-product-compliance
Lightning Source LLC
Chambersburg PA
CBHW020455100426
42813CB00031B/3375/J